Houses

and

Homes

Mike Jackson

Illustrated by

Jenny Mumford

Evans

This is our house.

4

People around the world live in lots of different sorts of houses.

Let's go and see some of them in the magic helicopter.

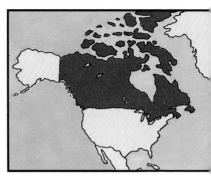

Now we have
landed near
to the North Pole, in
Canada.

This is where the Inuit
people live.

The Inuit build igloos to sleep
in when they go hunting.

*It must be
cold in there.*

It looks cold but it's really
warm and snug inside.

7

Now we are in the

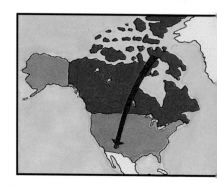

American South-west. Those homes belong to the Pueblo Indians.

They are adobe houses.

What does adobe mean?

Adobe are clay bricks that have been dried in the sun.

9

Now we're in
Zimbabwe,
in Africa.

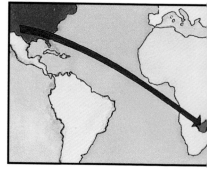

Look, these houses are made from mud and grass.

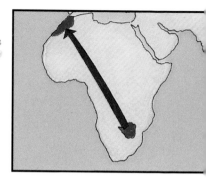

This is Morocco, in North Africa. The houses have flat roofs because there is very little rain.

The walls are thick and
the windows are small.

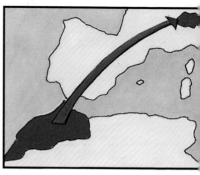

Now we are in the Swiss Alps. In Switzerland many people live in chalets with gently sloping roofs.

The snow stays on the roof and keeps the house warm.

They all have pretty balconies.

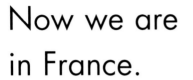

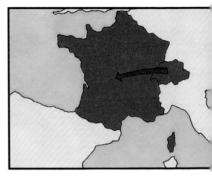

Now we are
in France.
Many thousands of years ago
people lived in these caves.

They painted pictures on
the walls.

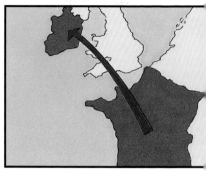

Now we are
in Ireland.

That caravan is used by
tourists. It used to be the
home of a
family of
gipsies.

It's painted in lovely colours.

This pretty thatched

cottage is in England. It was built 400 years ago.

21

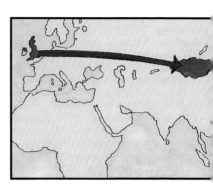

We are in
Mongolia.
Those round tents are called
yurts.

These people are called
nomads. They move from
place to place.

Now we are
in Japan.

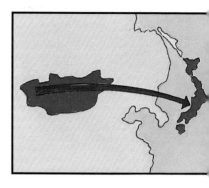

In this house the rooms
are divided by sliding
doors made out of paper.

24

25

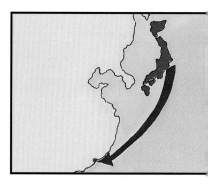

This is Hong Kong harbour. Many of the people in Hong Kong live on boats.

27

29

Here are some of the houses that the children saw on their journey. Can you remember where they are found?